ABORTION
Come now, and let us reason together.

By
Rick DeMichele, Pastor
Treasure Valley Baptist Church
Meridian, ID 83642
Copyright © 2010

Published by TVBC
1300 S. Teare Ave.
Meridian, ID 83642
(208) 888-4545
Please visit our web site at www.tvbc.org

DayStar Publishing
1-800-311-1823
www.daystarpublishing.com

2015 Editing and Cover Design
Truth and Song Christian Bookstore
www.truthandsong.com

ISBN 978-1-890120-67-2
Library of Congress: 2010940589

Special thanks are in order to several individuals who have helped make this booklet possible: Pastor Glenn Stocker for all the work and research he has done on the abortion issue including his booklet *What God Says About: Abortion Versus Pro-Life* Thanks also to Mrs. Stephanie Dalton, PA-C for her help with medical and scientific information, and to Pastor David Potts for his help with resource material and the first edition booklet cover design, and to Mrs. Vickie Steinbach whose help in formatting and layout in the first edition booklet was invaluable.

TABLE OF CONTENTS

INTRODUCTION

The purpose of this booklet is to encourage reasonable people to look at abortion from two different perspectives, and to see that both of these points of view agree on the primary concerns involved with the abortion issue. Our premise is simple, *That if based upon **Scriptural** and **Scientific** evidence we agree that every unborn child is a unique individual, then the destruction of that individual is just as wrong as the destruction of any unique individual reading this booklet.* We will provide **Scriptural Proof** to show that the unborn child is as complete in their spirit, soul, and body as they are after they are born, and that they are recognized as a living person by God and His people before birth. Then we will show **Scientific Proof** that life begins at conception, as any reputable scientist familiar with biology would certainly agree.

After examining the evidence from these two aspects, we will look at substantiating arguments for and against abortion, and answer each one from the Scriptures or science as appropriate.

We will conclude by showing to any unbiased person that abortion is murder and should be opposed by all.

CHAPTER ONE

Scriptural Proof

Rather than attempt to cover every verse in the Bible that deals with the subject, we will look at several of the more familiar passages.

Looking first at **Luke 1:41** we read,

"And it came to pass, that, when Elisabeth heard the salutation of Mary, the babe leaped in her womb; and Elisabeth was filled with the Holy Ghost and
Vs. 44 For lo, as soon as the voice of thy salutation sounded in mine ears, the babe leaped in my womb for joy."

In these two verses we see the babe in the woman (John the Baptist) doing things and being motivated just like a person. Notice he hears, he leaps, and pertaining to motivation, he leaps because of what he hears. In the first verse we have the narrative (*all scripture is given by inspiration of God...* **1 Timothy 3:16**) declaring these things so, and in the second verse,

Elisabeth, filled with the Holy Ghost restates the occurrence and gives human attributes to the child in her womb. While we are looking at this example, let us note verse fifteen of the same chapter prophesying of John,

"For he shall be great in the sight of the Lord, and shall drink neither wine nor strong drink; and he shall be filled with the Holy Ghost, even from his mother's womb (**Luke 1:15**)."

It certainly appears that mother and unborn babe were both filled with the Holy Ghost. This should be cause for any serious Bible student to ask: How could the Spirit of God fill the babe, if not human and not alive.

Turning our attention next to Acts 20:28, which shows that Jesus' blood was God's blood, we read in part, feed the church of God, which he hath purchased with his own blood. Since Leviticus 17:11, 14 tells us the life of the flesh is in the blood, then when Jesus had God's blood in Him, He was alive. When was this? It was while He was still in the womb of Mary. Jesus was alive in His physical body before He was actually born, His blood had developed by the sixth week of gestation.

John the Baptist and Jesus Christ are both unique individuals, but they were both born, and clearly from the scriptural perspective, both alive before they were born. There are several occasions in the scriptures where God gives a message to the mother of a baby before the child's birth, and it would be ridiculous to call them all special cases with regard to the issue of being living, unique individuals before their birth.

Next we read in **Genesis 16:11**

"And the angel of the LORD said unto her, Behold, thou art with child, and shalt bear a son, and thou shalt call his name Ishmael; because the LORD hath heard thy affliction."

Once again we see God's view on pregnancy. She is with *child*, she will bear a son, and she is told what to name her son.

Moving on to **Judges 13:3-7**

"And the angel of the LORD appeared unto the woman, and said unto her, Behold now, thou art barren, and bearest not: but thou shalt conceive, and bear a son. Now therefore beware, I pray thee, and drink not wine nor strong drink, and eat not any unclean thing: For, lo, thou shalt conceive, and bear a son; and no razor shall come on his head: for the child shall be a Nazarite unto God from the womb: and he shall begin to deliver Israel out of the hand of the Philistines. Then the woman came and told her husband, saying, A man of God came unto me, and his countenance was like the countenance of an angel of God, very terrible: but I asked him not whence he was, neither told me his name: But he said unto me, Behold thou shalt conceive, and bear a son; and now drink no wine nor strong drink, neither eat any unclean thing: for the child shall be a Nazarite to God from the womb to the day of his death."

Please note that Manoah's wife is told not to drink wine or strong drink because the child she was to bear would be a Nazarite from her womb. The law applied to the unborn child in this case. The unborn child is obviously alive or there would be no requirement to keep the law,

4

because we are told in **Romans 7:1** ...*that the law hath dominion over a man as long as he liveth.*

Next let us look at **Genesis 35:16-26**

"And they journeyed from Bethel; and there was but a little way to come to Ephrath: and Rachel travailed, and she had hard labour. And it came to pass, when she was in hard labour, that the midwife said unto her, Fear not; thou shalt have this son also. And it came to pass, as her soul was in departing, (for she died) that she called his name Benoni: but his father called him Benjamin. And Rachel died, and was buried in the way to Ephrath, which is in Bethlehem...Now the sons of Jacob were twelve: The sons of Leah; Reuben, Jacob's firstborn, and Simeon, and Levi, and Judah, and Issachar, and Zebulun: The sons of Rachel; Joseph, and Benjamin: And the sons of Bilhah, Rachel's handmaid; Dan and Naphtali: And the sons of Zilpah, Leah's handmaid; Gad and Asher: these are the sons of Jacob, which were born to him in Padanaram."

This passage deals with Jacob and his wives and sons leaving Padanaram and passing through Bethel on the way to Ephrath. Verse twenty-six tells us of his sons born to him in Padaranam, but Benjamin was born between Ephrath and Bethel. We can see in studying further that Benjamin was conceived in Padaranam, but born in the promised land, showing us how God looks upon the start of life. So, again we can see that God considered the boy Benjamin to be alive while in the womb of his mother.

We read in **Job 3:11** *Why died I not from the womb? Why did I not give up the ghost when I came out of the belly?* And in **Job 10:18**, *Wherefore then hast thou brought me forth out of the womb? Oh that I had given up the ghost, and no eye had seen me.* One would have to agree that you can only *give up the ghost* if you have one, and Job understood that he had his spirit even while he was in the womb. Since James 2:26 tells us the body without the spirit is dead, then the spirit is essential to life. The unborn child has a spirit, so he has a life; he has his own spirit, and his own life.

We can see the interaction of twins by looking at a couple of portions of scripture.

Genesis 25:22-26,

"And the children struggled together within her; and she said, If it be so, why am I thus? And she went to enquire of the LORD. And the LORD said unto her, Two nations are in thy womb, and two manner of people shall be separated from thy bowels; and the one people shall be stronger than the other people; and the elder shall serve the younger. And when her days to be delivered were fulfilled, behold there were twins in her womb. And the first cam out red, all over like an hairy garment; and they called his name Esau. And after that came his brother out, and his hand took hold on Esau's heel; and his name was Jacob: and Isaac was threescore years when she bare them."

And **Hosea 12:3,**

"He took his brother by the heel in the womb, and by his strength he had power with God."

These passages tell us about the struggle of Esau and Jacob **before** they were born. This struggle continued throughout their lives, and in fact throughout the lives of their posterity. The prophet Hosea speaking by the word of the Lord, tells us Jacob took his brother by the heel in the womb; that certainly indicates an independent will.

Psalm 139:13, 14,

"For thou hast possessed my reins: thou hast covered me in my mother's womb. I will praise thee; for I am fearfully and wonderfully made: marvelous are thy works; and that my soul knoweth right well.
Here David declares that God had covered **him** in his mother's womb."

Zechariah 12:1 tells us *...the LORD...formeth the spirit of man within him.* He does not breathe the spirit into him.

1 Samuel 4:19, 2 Samuel 11:5 and over two dozen other places we read about a mother *with child* when pregnant.

A strange chapter to the modern mind is **Exodus 21**. This is the oft quoted *eye for an eye* passage. The entire chapter is laying out various situations and the remedy for them at law; and in the midst of these we read in **verses 22-25,**

"If men strive, and hurt a woman with child, so that her fruit depart from her, and yet no mischief follow: he shall surely be punished, according as the woman's husband will lay upon him; and he shall pay as the judges determine. And if any mischief follow, then thou shalt give life for life, Eye for eye, tooth for tooth, hand for hand, foot for foot, Burning for burning, wound for wound, stripe for stripe."

This passage speaks about a woman's fruit departing from her (premature delivery) as a result of men striving. It gives the remedy for the situation in either of the two possible cases; *yet no mischief follow* and *if any mischief follow.* It is obvious that the man who hurt the woman is fined if *no mischief follow,* but less obvious to the reader is whether or not the baby survives. What is very clear however is the punishment in the case *if any mischief follow.* Where there is malicious intent to hurt either the baby or the mother, the guilty man will suffer the same injury he inflicted upon his victims, even to the point of capital punishment. The two cases are similar to how we differentiate today between manslaughter and premeditated murder. Note that the premeditated malicious case here, that is *if any mischief follow,* does not deal exclusively with the loss of life, but deals also with injury.

Having looked at these instances that clearly show the living state of the babe before birth, let us answer an erroneous teaching put forth by some who would use the Bible to deny this truth. Some have declared that *a baby is not alive until it breathes air on its own.*

This erroneous teaching is based upon **Genesis 2:7** which says, *And the **LORD** God formed man out of the dust of the ground, and breathed into his nostrils the breath of life; and man became a living soul.* While this is a beautiful passage to teach the trichotomy of man, it is a poor text to study the nature of the unborn baby. Adam was created as an adult, he was never a baby, nor was he born. So we can reason this is the wrong section of scripture to learn about the uniqueness of life in the unborn baby. We should also notice that when the **LORD** breathed on him and he became a living soul, he was spiritually alive as well, in fellowship with God. If we follow the narrative into the next chapter we observe that when Adam sinned and died spiritually, he did not quit breathing. Even after he became spiritually dead, the breath of life was still in his nostrils. We mention this fact because we read in **John 20:22** *And when he had said this, he breathed on them, and saith unto them, Receive ye the Holy Ghost.* It is obvious His breathing on them did not give them *physical* life, because they were already physically alive. So, when God breathed on Adam, he received spiritual life as noted by the phrase, *and man became a **living** soul.* So it refers not only to physical life, but also to spiritual life. To be sure, if you are deprived of air long enough, you will die, but an unborn child can be fully alive and fully human without breathing air through his nostrils, the oxygen is in his blood. As we saw before, **Leviticus 17:11** says *the life of the flesh is in the blood.* The blood is the vehicle which carries the oxygen around in the body, and an unborn child has his **own** blood, and therefore has his own life with spirit, soul and body.

CHAPTER TWO

Scientific Proof

The scientific argument against abortion must begin by addressing the question of when life begins. If it is determined that the developing embryo represents a unique human life, then the voluntary destruction of that life is unquestionably murder.

Before determining when life begins, we must determine what life is. We all have a concept of what constitutes life, but Webster defines life as *an organic entity with the ability to take in food, adapt to the environment, grow, and reproduce.*[1] The developing embryo absolutely demonstrates the first three characteristics with the future potential to reproduce.

Since ancient times the beginning of human life has been debated. However, the consensus among scientists, physicians, and embryologists is that life begins at conception. During the U.S. judicial subcommittee meeting on the Constitution in 1981, physicians supporting either abortion or the sanctity of life were asked to testify concerning when life begins. Not a single physician testified to anything other than that life begins at conception. Consider the following statements made by physicians during this meeting.

Dr. Alfred M. Bonioanni, professor of pediatrics and obstetrics at the University of Pennsylvania, stated,

"I have learned from my earliest medical education that human life begins at the time of conception...I submit that human life is precious throughout this entire sequence, from conception to adulthood, and that any interruption at any point through out this time constitutes a termination of human life..."2

Professor Micheline Matthews-Roth, Harvard University Medical School says

"It is incorrect to say that biological data cannot be decisive...**It is scientifically correct to say that an individual human life begins at conception...** Our laws, one function of which is to preserve the lives of our people, should be based upon accurate scientific data."3

Conception refers to a moment in time called fertilization when the nuclei of a sperm and an ovum unite with each contributing twenty-three chromosomes to form a unique individual. At that moment the cell contains all of the information necessary for a new life. Hair color, eye color, height, gender, skin color, propensity for certain disease, blood type and numerous other features are set. This single cell is incapable of developing into anything other than a human being and will proceed until death occurs through natural or violent means. The significance of this event is echoed in embryology textbooks. The authors of *Human Embryology and Teratology* state that…

"Although human life is a continuous process, fertilization is a critical landmark because, under ordinary circumstances, a new, genetically distinct human organism is thereby formed."[4]

The developmental geneticist Jerome Lejeune (1926-1994) who discovered the chromosomal basis for Down's Syndrome, clearly stated the magnitude of fertilization.

14

"...each of us has a unique beginning, the moment of conception...As soon as the 23 chromosomes carried by the sperm encounter the 23 chromosomes carried by the ovum, the whole information necessary and sufficient to spell out all the characteristics of the new being is gathered...a new human being is defined which has never occurred before and will never occur again...[it] is not just simply a nondescript cell, or a 'population' or loose 'collection' of cells, but a very specialized individual..."5

Following fertilization the cell begins to rapidly divide in the uterine wall of the mother. From that time forward the child is an entirely discrete entity from the mother, separated by a barrier called the placenta. Though the developing embryo is *renting space* from the mother, this growing collection of cells cannot be called part of the mother; they are genetically different and have separate organ systems.

In the days and weeks following conception amazing changes occur quickly in the embryo. The fetal heart begins to form eighteen days following conception with a measurable heart beat by twenty-one to twenty-four days after fertilization. The fetal brain begins to develop on day twenty-five. Brain waves can be detected by day forty after fertilization. Eyes are present in a rudimentary form by seven weeks following conception and arms and legs appear the following week. By the end of the tenth week all parts necessary for life have formed. It is sobering that these features along with many others are present at about the time of many first trimester abortions.

The argument is often made that because the unborn child cannot live independent of the mother that it does not constitute a separate autonomous individual. However, that is merely stating that the child is dependent on an outside source for nutrition, warmth, and protection. This is equally true of a newborn, a one-year-old child, a Quadriplegic, a mentally challenged adult, or a comatose adult. That a child cannot live autonomously, particularly in the early weeks of gestation does not negate the validitye of the life.

Unrestricted abortion is legal in most states during the first and second trimesters. However, the youngest premature infant known to survive is Amilia Taylor, delivered in 2007 in Miami, Florida at 22 weeks, 6 days gestation weighing only 10 ounces. She went home four months later weighing four pounds. Certainly this illustrates in the extreme that life apart from the mother is possible during the second trimester of pregnancy. Thus, voluntary termination of this same infant is not the disposal of the *products of conception* or a *potential human life*, but rather intentional murder.

We have taken time to define life and to determine that life begins at the moment of conception. How then would death be defined? The medical and legal communities have established that a person can be declared *brain dead* when there is an irreversible end of brain activity (including involuntary activity necessary to sustain life) following loss of blood flow and oxygenation. While this may seem pedantic, death can only occur where there has been life. Brain activity, oxygenation, and blood flow are all present in a developing embryo by forty days following fertilization. Certainly the voluntary cessation of these functions would then be considered the killing of a living being.

Thus, modern science concludes that life begins at conception. Murder as defined in the Encarta Dictionary6 is *to kill another person deliberately and not in self-defense or with any other extenuating circumstance recognized by law, or to kill somebody with great violence and brutality.* Abortion then, is synonymous with murder.

Following the Nuremberg Medical Trials, the Geneva Declaration of Physicians was written in response to the medical atrocities committed by the Nazi regime. The Declaration states: *I will maintain the utmost respect for human life, from the time of its **conception, even under threat.** I will not use my medical knowledge contrary to the laws of humanity.*7

It seems that the 1973 Roe v. Wade decision overturned our common sense. We can define life, death, and murder and then look away while 1.5 million innocents are slaughtered. What is at the root, money, situational ethics, convenience, pride?

CHAPTER TWO – SCIENTIFIC PROOF

CHAPTER THREE

Supporting Arguments

There are many arguments on both sides of the abortion issue, and both sides appeal to the moral question of *what is right*. Having already looked at our **Scriptural** and **Scientific Proofs** against abortion, we will now examine the more popular arguments in favor of abortion. We will look at as many of these arguments as time and space will allow, but let us pause to remind ourselves that real morality, and the true standard of right is found in the revelation from God called the Bible. Within that revelation, we find records of terrible injustices and atrocities when *every man did that which was right in his own eyes* (**Judges 17:6**).

Some of the more popular arguments used to support abortion are:

* A Woman's Right to Choose
* Save the Life of the Mother
* A Mother Can't Cope with Raising a Baby & The Unwanted Child

* A Child with Disabilities
* Economic Difficulties
* The Majority of Americans Favor Abortion
* A Child from Rape
* To Reduce Disease
* To Reduce Exploding Population Growth

A Woman's Right to Choose

While abortion advocates talk about the many reasons abortion is necessary for the good of our society, recent surveys suggest that *three quarters of women indicated that they were concerned about how a baby would change their life by interfering with their job, schooling, or responsibilities in caring for others.*1 Thus we see that abortion is the death of a child for the mere convenience of the mother seventy-five percent of the time. When a doctor is involved in ending a pregnancy, the matter is settled between a woman and her doctor, and in that case the choice of living or dying is stripped away from the unborn child, while the choice of convenience is granted to the mother.

Notice also that roughly half of all babies are female, and these young females have no choice regarding their bodies under the *pro-choice* façade, but are murdered and destroyed for the sake of feminism's most sacred sacrament. This same point is made by abortion researcher Kent Kelly

"In many circles, feminists rally to the pro-abortion cause as another expression of women's rights...If the cause is the glory of womanhood, why is it selective women's rights instead of protecting all women equally?"2

A woman's right to choose begins with the choice not to become pregnant.

Save the Life of the Mother

Another argument proposed in favor of abortion is that they must sometimes kill the baby in order to save the life of the mother. This however, is an emotionally charged attempt to coerce those who disagree with abortion to surrender a portion of their reasoning to the adversary. Many politicians, so as not to appear uncaring, readily cave in to the pressure of the pro-abortion special interest groups by including *life of the mother* clauses in legislative drafts. Certainly the pro-life perspective is pro-life in regard to the mother as well, believing that medical professionals should strive to protect **all** life. Dr. Joseph P. Donnelly is someone who deals with this on a regular basis. Dr. Donnelly was medical director of Margaret Hague Hospital in New Jersey, and from 1947 to 1961 there were 115,000 deliveries at his maternity hospital with no abortions. Dr. Donnelly says

"Abortion is never necessary to save the life of the mother."[3]

Dr. Bernard J. Pisani, Professor of Obstetrics and Gynecology at the New York University School of Medicine says

"Medical reasons for provoking abortion are just about non-existent. In fact, no basis on pure medical grounds ever really stands up."[4]

Again, Dr. John L. Grady, former Chief of Staff at Glades General Hospital in Florida says

"Thousands of physicians across the United States, each of whom has cared for hundreds of mothers and infants during their respective years of practice, state firmly they have never in these thousands of pregnancies seen a single instance where the life of the infant had to be sacrificed to save the mother, nor have they seen a situation where a mother has been lost for failure of the physician to perform an abortion. In fact, in more than thirteen years of obstetrical practice, I never lost a mother from any cause. Moreover, during that time, at the public hospital where I was staff member there were thousands of babies delivered and, to my knowledge, not a single therapeutic abortion. Thus, with today's advanced medical knowledge and practice, a 'therapeutic' abortion is never necessary, because competent physicians, using the latest medical and surgical techniques, can preserve the lives of both the mother and the child."[5]

Also, Dr. Roy S. Hefferman of Tufts University, speaking to the congress of the American College of Surgeons, says

"Anyone who performs a therapeutic abortion is either ignorant of modern methods of treating the complications of pregnancy or is unwilling to take the time to use them."6

With modern medical science and technology available to us, the *save the mother* argument can be seen for the emotional manipulation that it really is.

A Mother Can't Cope with Raising a Baby & The Unwanted Child

It is reasonable to consider these two arguments at the same time since the logic of each is answered by the same simple solution. There are hundreds of people who can cope with, and do want a child to raise and share their lives with. Anyone who cares to research the adoption process will find that THERE ARE NO UNWANTED CHILDREN. There are many people who want to adopt a baby, and the long waiting periods are evidence of the sincerity of the multitudes who are looking for a child that they can call their own. If a woman feels overwhelmed with the prospects of parenthood and unable to cope with that responsibility, it is no reason to end the pregnancy and destroy the child. After the baby is born, an adoption can relieve the birth mother of those burdens and grant to the adoptive parents the joy and expectations that accompany their baby. Having looked at the first solution we can examine a second alternative. In most instances, *I don't want this baby,* or *I can't cope with raising a baby* usually means *I don't want to be pregnant right now.* Many mothers do step up to their responsibilities with joy and gratitude for the gift of life once their baby is born. Dr. Edward Lenoski of the university of California states

"An unwanted pregnancy in the early months does not necessarily mean an unwanted baby after delivery."7

You can be sure that **someone** wants that baby!

A Child with Disabilities

What a sad thing to promote the destruction of children who might not *measure up* physically or mentally.

Addressing the American Psychological Association Meeting, Dr. D. Van Hoeck states

"Though it may be common and fashionable to believe that the malformed enjoys life less than the normal, this appears to lack both empirical and theoretical support."8

Each of us has a desire to enjoy life, regardless of whether one measures up to or falls short of *perfection*.

The truth of the matter is that individuals with disabilities can and do enjoy their lives.

A mother of a Down's Syndrome child, Mrs. Delahoyde devotes herself to fighting against infant euthanasia and abortion. Her belief is that in modern society, everything is geared toward perfection. Some think that death might be the best option for some handicapped children because they think real people are *normal* people.

In fact, when looking at the research one sees in *The Journal of Marriage and Family, Abortion of Defective Fetuses: Attitudes of Congenitally*

Impaired Children, by Naomi Breslau No. 49, Pg. 840, that …

"The public's devaluation of the potential lives of handicapped fetuses is regarded as an aspect of its negative attitude toward handicapped persons, an attitude that presupposes that their lives must be unhappy and miserable. In contrast to this general view, it is argued that *there is remarkable joy and happiness in the lives of most handicapped children* and that *their entrance into a family is frequently looked back upon in subsequent years as an extraordinary positive experience.* Parents of disabled children are said to view their child *as a human being first and a handicapped only secondary.* The implication here is that parents of disabled children will be less inclined than other parents to approve of abortion of defective fetuses."9

Another thing to remember regarding aborting a baby for the sake of disabilities is that very often the doctors are wrong about their prognosis of the baby's problems. That is to say that often they are not disabled at all, or may have only a slight defect compared to the early diagnosis. There is very little research done on this subject because it exposes some of the medical community to significant liabilities. While it may be unclear what percentage of babies are destroyed for the sake of misdiagnosis, there are abundant examples of survivors who are leading productive lives. Consider the case of Tim Tebow.

University of Florida quarterback Tim Tebow won U.S. college football's highest honor...If his mother had followed her doctor's advice when she was carrying him, he would be just another abortion statistic.

Tim's parents, Bob and Pam Tebow, moved to the Philippines in 1985 to conduct a Christian missionary outreach. While pregnant with Tim, Pam contracted amoebic dysentery through contaminated drinking water. Her doctor told her that the medications she needed to recover would result in irreversible damage to the child she was carrying. She was advised to have an abortion. She refused. Tim was born healthy and robust in 1987. His mother described him as *skinny, but rather long*. Today he stands six-foot-three, weighs 235 pounds, and has been described as a physical and athletic phenomenon. 10

Economic Difficulties

Economic difficulties will always exist, to quote Jesus Christ, *For ye have the poor with you always.* (**Mark 14:7**). For most of human history, the majority of people raising families have had economic difficulties. The question is not one of economics, but of morals, and we cannot justify the destruction of babies (before birth or after), on economic grounds without becoming party to a crime. This is a ridiculous defense of abortion, as there are multiple programs with private or government funding to help those struggling financially.

Dr. Susan Dudley, PhD writing for the National Abortion Federation states
For example, many women who are denied funding for abortion have one anyway, usually at great sacrifice to themselves and their families.11

It is more reasonable for a woman to make great financial sacrifices to save her child's life than to kill her baby. Dr. Dudley goes on to point out that they may take on extra work.

The Majority of Americans Favor Abortion

We are often told that the majority of Americans favor abortion. It is more probable that most Americans take a middle position on the issue, and can be swayed toward either position by an impassioned activist. With all the debate raging, there are still some points to consider about the argument. First, the issue has never been put to a popular vote. Second, it is unreasonable to think of an innocent life being ended on the simple basis of a majority vote. Third, the reason our founding fathers set up a democratic republic was to have *Rule of Law* which allows the people their voice, but protects the minority from mob rule.

Abortion researcher Kent Kelly states

"If the right to life may be eliminated on the basis of public sentiment, then any other right may be taken away by majority decision. No right is more basic. No right is more obvious. Only someone on the brink of insanity would want his right to live put to a vote of the majority."12

A Child from Rape

Dealing with the aftermath of rape is difficult and emotional. Rape is a terrible thing, so bad in fact that some states still list it as a capital crime. Whether a rapist should be executed or not is the topic of another debate, but to automatically execute an innocent child before it is born is not justice. Murdering the baby but only putting the rapist in prison punishes the baby more severely than the criminal.

To use the argument of how to deal with children resulting from rape to support abortion is a stretch within itself, especially since the situation rarely occurs.

Dr. F.D. Mecklenburg, M.D. states

"Although frequently cited by pro-abortionists, pregnancies resulting from rape are so rare as to be virtually non-existent. There are several contributing factors to this. In addition to the pure mathematical odds against pregnancy resulting from a single random act, medical research indicates that an extremely high percentage of women exposed to severe emotional trauma will not ovulate. The rape itself, therefore acts as a psychological *birth control*."13

Dr. J. Kuchera, M.D. writing for the Journal of the American Medical Association states

"A scientific study of one thousand cases of rape treated medically immediately after the rape results in zero cases of pregnancies.14
As awful as rape is, it should not be the determining factor in the abortion issue, and should not be the grounds for destroying an innocent baby."

To Reduce Disease

The disease reduction argument promoted by the pro-abortion special interest groups is more argumentative than reasonable. Using medical and scientific terminology they go on in filibuster fashion expecting no one to check the facts or the logic of their conclusions.

Dr. Hymie Gorden, Chairman of the Dept. of Medical Genetics, Mayo Clinic, Minnesota says

"Talk about breeding out genetic diseases is a lot of nonsense. Seriously affected persons are unlikely to marry and have children; the genes are passed along by carriers. For instance, there are forty carriers for every person with sickle cell anemia...if every victim of this disease were eliminated, it would require seven hundred and fifty years just to cut the incidence in half; to stamp it out altogether would require two hundred thousand abortions for every five hundred thousand couples. Because each 'normal' person is the carrier of three or four bad genes, the only way to eliminate genetic diseases would be to sterilize or abort everybody."15

Consider a familiar lecture in medical schools regarding the students' recommendation to abort. In this particular case, the college professor explains that the father had syphilis, and the mother had TB. They had four children already. One was blind, one was born dead, one was a deaf mute and another had TB. The mother was pregnant with her fifth child. Almost without exception, the medical students recommended abortion. To this the professor replied, *Congratulations! You have just killed BEETHOVEN!*16

Dr. C. Everett Koop, M.D., former Surgeon General of the United States, and former Surgeon-in-Chief of the Children's Hospital of Philadelphia says

When doctors are willing to become social executioners for millions of babies, we must examine what motives are used to justify their actions. Usually, the reasons given include preserving the life of the mother, the expectation of a defective child, rape, and incest. Even if these were valid reasons, they would account for only three percent of all abortions. A full ninety-seven percent of occur for matters of convenience and economy.17

Convenience and economy are the hidden forces behind the abortion industry. Young people are growing into adulthood with the notion that they can do as they please and not be faced with consequences. The ridiculous disease reduction argument serves as a flimsy shield both to those who perform abortions and those who have them, while ignoring the sanctity of life.

To Reduce Exploding Population Growth

Another argument vaunted by pro-abortionists is the *Population Explosion* Myth, which sounds more like Chicken Little declaring that the sky is falling than a reason to kill 1.5 million babies each year.

Dr. Dennis L. Cuddy, Ph.D. states,

"Today we constantly hear about the suffering people of an overly crowded India. While there is little doubt that many people in India do suffer from a lack of food, this is not necessarily because of the number inhabiting that vast land. India has less people per square mile than England, West Germany or Taiwan... There is actually not a 'population problem' as such today, as all the people of the world could fit side-by-side into greater Jacksonville, Florida. What we have is a problem of food distribution and the availability of natural resources."18

Nick Eberstadt of Harvard's Center for Population Studies found that

"The world's population growth peaked at 1.9% around 1970 and is now down to 1.7%. In Western Europe the growth rate has dropped 50%, in North America 30%, in China 30%, and in India 10%. Interestingly, demographer Donald Bogue in a Population Reference Bureau paper estimated that only 4.7% of the decline in the world fertility rate could be attributed to family planning efforts. Currently, the U.S. fertility rate is 1.7 (a rate of 2.1 is necessary to maintain a population replacement level). And the decline in fertility in this country is most pronounced among blacks, American Indians and Mexican-Americans (25% of Native American women have been sterilized by monies earmarked by the treaty agreement for medical needs, and 35% of all Puerto Rican women have been sterilized)."19

Such a remarkable decrease in the birth rate portends a disproportionate population of aged citizens in contrast to the diminished ranks of our youth. The enormous economic burden this will put on the younger generation in supporting our seniors will foster and increase avocation of euthanasia, which could proceed unchallenged among a newly emerging electorate freshly indoctrinated in the idea that life is cheap.

It is easy to see the fallacy of this argument. Dividing the total land mass of the world by the six billion people on the planet would give everyone about six and one-eighth acres each, and everyone (rounded to six billion) on the planet could stand inside the city limits of Jacksonville, Florida (874.3 square miles) with a little over four square feet per person. The planet is not as crowded as some would have us think, and crowding is certainly no reason to kill our children.

Perhaps the leading force in population control is Planned Parenthood, whose Margaret Sanger advocated situational ethics and birth control *to create a race of thoroughbreds* (*Birth Control Review*, November 1921). This forerunner of Hitler's eugenics movement also proclaimed that *the most merciful thing that the large family does to one of its infant members is to kill it* (*Women and the New Race*). Today Planned Parenthood does not use such forceful language, but rather more subtle terminology, like advocating the need for *genetic counseling*.[20]

According to a supplement to **Family Planning Perspectives** published by Planned Parenthood entitled, *Examples of Proposed Measures to Reduce U.S. Fertility, by universality or Selectivity of Impact*:

1) Universal Impact
Restructure family, encourage increased homo sexuality, educate for family limitation, fertility control agents in the water supply, encourage women to work.

2) Economic Impact
Tax policies: marriage tax, child tax, additional on parents with more than one or two children in school.

3) Social Impact
Compulsory sterilization of all who have two children except for a few who would be allowed three, confine childbearing to a limited number of adults, stock certificate type permits for children, discouragement of private home ownership, stop awarding housing on the basis of family size.

4) Measures Predicted on Existing Motivations
Payments to encourage sterilization, abortion and contraception, along with allowing certain contraceptives to be distributed non-medically.21
It is a sad state of affairs when Planned Parenthood gets grants and subsidies from the government to carry out these and other programs. Programs such as school based health clinics, where a young girl can get transportation to an abortion clinic without parental knowledge or consent, have an abortion, and return to class the same day with no one knowing, but a few school officials.

To sum up the first three chapters, it is clear that:

•Scripturally the unborn child, the fetus, is a unique individual human being.
•Scientifically the unborn child, the fetus, is a unique individual human being.
•The arguments used to support abortion ignore or deny that the unborn child, the fetus, is a unique individual being.

•Convenience and economics are the real reasons for today's proliferation of abortion.

•Abortion at best is manslaughter and more often murder.

CHAPTER FOUR

Conclusion

Come now, and let us reason together, saith the LORD: though your sins be as scarlet, they shall be as white as snow; though they be red like crimson, they shall be as wool. Isaiah 1:18

We have seen Scripturally that abortion is murder. We have seen Scientifically that abortion is murder. We have seen that the only way to make an argument for abortion is to pretend that the unborn child is not a child at all; or to admit that he is, but allow that his life is of no value until some arbitrary judgment is made at some random time giving him the same privilege of life that the rest of us enjoy. The thing that we must now consider is what will we do with these facts.

To begin with, let us do what we can to help those who may feel like the circumstances of life have left them no other alternative. There are alternatives. There are Crisis Pregnancy Centers in many cities across our nation. There are families that desperately want a baby. There are people who are willing to help someone give their baby a life. Let us do what we can to give hope to the hopeless.

Do not let the lie *it's not a baby 'til after it's born* go unchallenged. Educate your own children. This is not a decision for them to make when they are faced with the

crisis in their own life. You would not let a six-year old decide IF he wants to get an education, nor do you let a sixteen-year-old decide which side of the road he wants to drive on; and you should not let your young adolescents decide about sexual activity and the consequences of it based only on what they may have picked up at school. Teach your children about these things. Teach your community about the unborn. Use situations of pregnant women in your community to springboard into conversations about how developed the baby is at various ages of gestation, and about how a baby may react to different stimuli. Be a voice for the unborn. That does not require you to become a zealous activist, just someone who will challenge the lie when they hear it.

COME NOW, AND LET US REASON TOGETHER

A further consideration of the facts before us would prompt us to be kind and forgiving to those shattered women who live with the regret of an abortion. We titled this booklet **Abortion: Come Now, and Let Us Reason Together** because God wants you to stop and see how He can forgive you of your sins. God is holy, but He is also love, and in His love He can be just, and the justifier of the unjust through His Son Jesus Christ. He says *though your sins be as scarlet, they shall be white as snow* (**Isaiah 1:18**). If you have had an abortion, there is forgiveness with the Lord. And when the Lord forgives a repentant sinner, He washes away the guilt with the sin.

While we are considering the forgiveness of the sin of abortion, we should make the point clear to all who read this, that the grounds for God forgiving abortion is the same for Him forgiving all other sins, the Gospel of Jesus Christ. As we look at a couple of Bible verses that tell us the Gospel simply, notice that forgiveness is not the property of a church or denomination, nor is it found in a philosophy.

The Bible tells us in **1 Corinthians 15:3,4**

"...how that Christ died for our sins according to the scriptures; And that he was buried, and that he rose again the third day according to the scriptures."

You see, Jesus Christ took the punishment for our sins. God can now offer forgiveness based on Christ's death, burial, and resurrection. The Bible states very plainly in **Romans 6:23** *The wages of sin is death; but the gift of God is eternal life through Jesus Christ our Lord.* Since Jesus Christ paid that penalty, those who receive Him by faith as their Savior do not have a penalty to pay. We can make the application of that payment through faith as we are told in **Ephesians 2:8, 9** *For by grace are ye saved through faith; and that not of yourselves: it is the gift of God: Not of works, lest and man should boast.*

Believe that He died for you and ask Him in prayer to accept you, and He will not only wash away your sins, but also give you everlasting life. Don't you think it is reasonable that if

Christ loved you enough to die for your sins, He wants to forgive you?

If you have already had an abortion, or have participated in performing an abortion there is cleansing and forgiveness with the Lord. The forgiveness of God comes to you through the love of God. Remember, *For God so loved the world, that he gave his only begotten son, that whosoever believeth in him should not perish but have everlasting life* (**John 3:16**).

Since God loves you that much, He shed His own blood to pay for all your sins. The Bible tells us in

Hebrews 9:14,

"How much more shall the blood of Christ, who through the eternal Spirit offered himself without spot to God, **purge your conscience** from dead works to serve the living God?"

And also in **1 John 1:7,**

"But if we walk in the light, as he is in the light, we have fellowship one with another, and the blood of Jesus Christ his Son **cleanseth us from**

all   **sin**.

You can be cleansed and have your conscience purged from the memory of your sins. There are many churches and pregnancy support groups that are willing to help you, but more than that, Jesus Christ is waiting to help you, waiting for you to turn to Him, and in a humble and contrite spirit receive from Him the forgiveness and cleansing He offers.

You can pray a simple prayer such as this, *Oh God, I know that I am a sinner. I believe Jesus was my substitute when He died on the Cross. I believe His shed blood, death and resurrection were for me. I now receive Him as my Savior. I thank You for the forgiveness of my sins, the gift of salvation and everlasting life, because of your merciful grace. Amen.*

HELP FOR THOSE IN AN UNPLANNED PREGNANCY

Birthright International
800-550-4900
www.birthright.org

Birthright provides caring, non-judgmental support to girls and women who are distressed by an unplanned pregnancy. Using its own resources and those of the community, Birthright offers positive and loving alternatives. Birthright presents many services and refers for many more. They provide friendship and emotional support, free pregnancy testing, and maternity and baby clothes. They also give information and referrals to help clients meet legal, medical, financial, and housing needs. Birthright treats each women as an individual who deserves kindness and respect, as well as personal attention to her unique situation. All Birthright services are absolutely free, absolutely confidential, and available to any woman regardless of age, race, creed, economic or marital status.

Additional Information
Right to Life
(202) 626-8800
www.nrlc.org

Idaho Chooses Life
(208) 344-8709
www.idahochooseslife.
org

END NOTES

Chapter 1
All references as cited out of the King James Bible

Chapter 2
1. Webster's New World Compact Desk Dictionary
Second Edition, 2002 Hungry Minds, Inc. Ohio
2. Hearings before the Constitution Subcommittee of the Senate Judiciary Committee. *Constitutional Amendments Relating to Abortion.* 97th Congress, 1st Session (1981). 2 Vols. Serial No. J-97-62.
3. Ibid
4. O'Rahilly, Ronan and Muller, Fabiola. Human
embryology and Teratology, 2nd edition. New York: Wiley- Liss, 1996, p. 8.
5. Lejeune, J. A symphony of the preborn child: part 2. Hagerstown, MD: NAACP; 1989
6. **Encarta®** World English Dictionary [North American Edition] © & 2009 Microsoft Corporation

7. The Geneva Conventions of 1949. In Human Rights Documents. Pp 325-461, Washington DC U.S. Government Printing Office, 1983

Chapter 3

1. Torres and Darroch, Family Planning Perspectives, Vol. 20, No. 4, pp. 169
Stable   URL:
http://www.jstor.org/stable/2135792

2. Kent Kelly, Abortion, (Southern Pines: Calvary Press,1981), p. 89

3. Ibid, p. 94

4. Ibid, p. 95

5. Ibid, p. 96

6. Ibid, p. 94

7. Ibid, p. 78

8. Ibid, p. 79

9. Journal of Marriage and of the Family, Abortion of Defec tive Fetuses: Attitudes of Mothers of Congeniality Im paired Children, by Naomi Breslau No. 49 p. 840

10. Thaddeua M. Baklinski, (LifeSiteNews.com) Dec. 11, 2007

11. Susan Dudley, Economics of Abortion, National Abortion Federation, 2003, p2

12. Kelly, p. 90

13. Ibid, p. 78
14. Ibid, p. 79
15. Ibid, p.80
16. Ibid, p. 13
17. Ibid, p. 83
18. Kelly p. 115, citing Dr. D.L. Cuddy, Ph.D. National Pro-Life Journal, Fairfax, Virginia
19. Kelly, p. 116
20. Ibid, pp. 119,120
21. Ibid, pp. 120,121

Chapter 4
All references as cited out of the King James Bible

Made in the USA
Columbia, SC
15 May 2018